Floristry
Basics
Materials

Floristry
Basics
Materials

Creations Rita Van Gansbeke
Text Patricia De Corte
Photography Isabelle Persyn

Funded by
MISSION COLLEGE
Carl D. Perkins Vocational and Technical Education Act Grant

stichting
kunstboek

Floral materials
take you back to the source
inviting you to a creative,
fascinating meeting
between purity and beauty.

Discover and enjoy.

Rita Van Gansbeke
Patricia De Corte
Isabelle Persyn

Contents

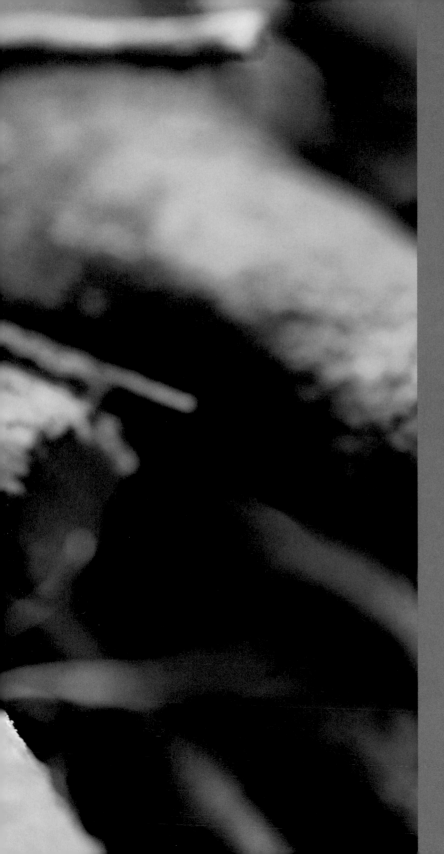

Roots

The root is a vital, usually subterranean part of a plant. Indispensable for the absorption of water and nutrition, it is a true vegetable anchor. In flower arranging, roots have an added value, as the sometimes whimsical shapes represent a real creative challenge to produce experimental flower arrangements.

10 Vanda orchid aerial roots

2 little porcelain beads

Thin silver wire

Cold glue

Flexible aluminium wire

to serve as a chain

Roll up the aerial roots from the inside out to form a flat-surfaced plate. Fix with silver wire after a few wrappings. Make a new circle with a second root. Glue this one to the first plate. This will give your creation some depth. Clasp a little bead onto the heart of the arrangement. Fasten the two shapes together with silver wire and attach them to the chain.

Vanda root necklace

TIP Use fresh aerial roots which are easy to process.

Floating wreath of tropical roots

Bind tropical roots together in parallel on the double metal ring using floral wire.
Clasp six little pieces of wet floral foam in a jute jacket filled with plastic foil.
Arrange the various green materials and the roses.

Tropical roots

Hydrangea macrophylla/hydrangea

Euonymus europaeus/spindle tree

Sambucus nigra/elderberry

Rubus 'Chester'/blackberry

Nigella damascena 'Damos'/love-in-a-mist

Anethum graveolens/dill

Rosa 'Old Dutch'

Rosa 'Sweet Avalance'

Rosa 'Milca Sensation'

Floral wire

Jute

Plastic foil

Floral foam

Double metal ring on four

welded reinforcing bars

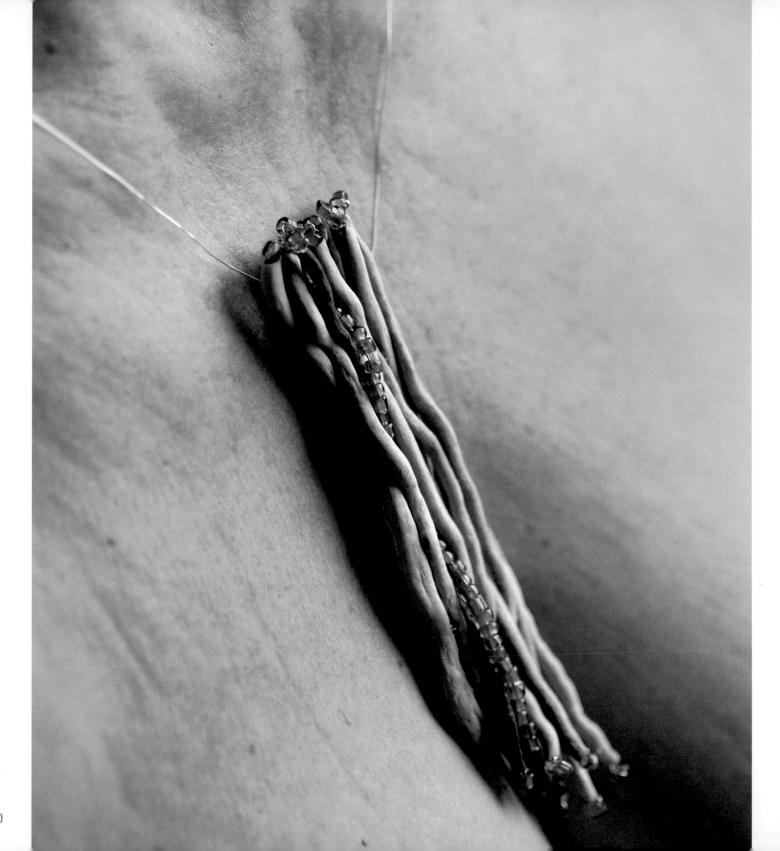

10 little Vanda orchid aerial roots (length 15 cm)

Glass beads

Thin silver wire

Cold glue

Vanda root pendant

Thread the aerial roots in parallel on a silver wire. Perform this operation in two places. Trim them to the same length at the top and to different lengths at the bottom. Put beads on a wire. Drench them in cold glue for a little while and put them on the root tips. Finish with a row of beads, which have been threaded on wire beforehand.

TIP You can store orchid roots in a sealed container in the freezer. Allow the roots to defrost in the sealed container before you start your flower arranging.

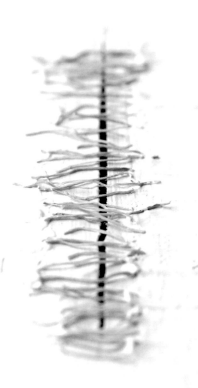

Rootlets of:

Allium porrum/leek

Raphanus sativus/winter radish

White and black gouache

Cutter

Cold glue

Canvas (2 pieces of 18 x 25 cm)

Canvas with roots

Rub white paint into a canvas with vertical strokes. Make an incision in the middle using a cutter. Apply little dots of cold glue along the edges of the incision. Distribute the leek rootlets right across the incision. Finish by applying horizontal whisks of paint to the root tips. Do exactly the same with the other canvas using black paint and winter radish rootlets.

9 Zea mays/maize plants

7 maize cob covering bracts

Floral wire

Sand

Terracotta pot

Terracotta with prop roots

TIP Do not collect the maize plants from the field just like that. Ask the maize grower for permission.

Fill the terracotta pot with sand. Clean the roots of the maize plants in water. Cut every plant into three. Put the pieces of stalk in the middle of the pot. Arrange the parts of the stalks with the roots up against the edge of the pot. Every root thus becomes a holder for rolled-up pieces of corn silk and little balls of root fibres, shaped with floral wire. Finish using covering bracts of the maize cobs.

Stems &
Branches

The stems carry the plants' leaves, flowers and fruits. They are not the same thing as the stalks, which are a connection between the plant and the stem. The leafstalks are part of the leaves.

Branches are woody stems. Their scars, nodes, buds and textures are pure eye-catchers, both in nature and in floral art works.

Broken stems of Helianthus rigidus/prairie sunflower

(2 sizes: 5 cm and 16 cm long)

Floral clay brick

4 thin iron bars

Floral wire

TIP If you place the clay brick with the iron bars on a rotating plate, it will be much easier to work all around the creation. This trick is also very practical if you want to make a Biedermeier.

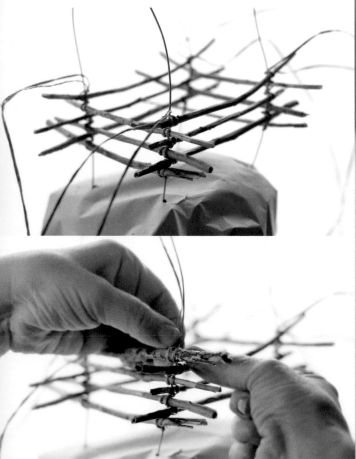

Whirling Structure with Prairie Sunflower

Stick four thin iron bars into the corners of a clay brick. Fix a double piece of floral wire on each iron stick with a turning movement. Build a structure with prairie sunflower stems, adding them two by two (first two long branches, then two short ones). Fix the stems each time at two points with floral wire. Once your creation is finished, remove the clay.

Linum usitatissimum/flax

Matricaria chamomilla/camomile

Pipettes

Flax Sheaf

Arrange the camomile into a linear bundle.
Place the stems in water-filled pipettes.
Bind the flax sheaf around the camomile
and fix with a knot of flax.

TIP Before you start arranging the plants,
remove all the roots from the flax and all
the leaves from the stems with your hands.

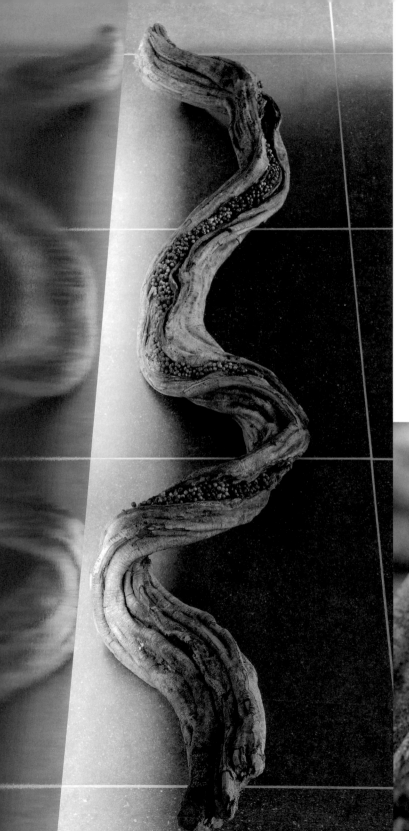

Chodondendron tomentosum/liane

Dry Schinus molle/pepper berries

Liane Snake

Clasp dry pepper berries into the grooves of
a piece of liane. Arrange the creation in such
a way that it has a fluent line. Where necessary,
you can glue the pepper berries onto the liane.

Cornus alba

Floral wire

Cornus Curtain

Make circles of different diameters with fresh
Cornus branches. Bind the far ends twice with floral
wire to keep the nice, round shape. Create a new
circle each time within the previous one.
For the long curtain mat, cut the Cornus branches
at equal lengths and bind them twice with floral
wire (see the technique described in 'River of
Cluster Roses' in the chapter 'Flowers').

TIP The Cornus
curtain is a gorgeous
alternative to the
traditional wallpaper.

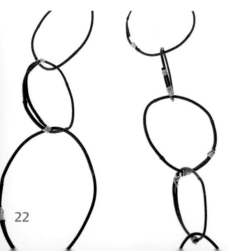

Little Potato Men

Solanum tuberosum 'Franceline'/potatoes

Rosa 'Old Dutch'

Rusty iron wire

Cut the potatoes into little pot shapes and hollow them out completely. Turn the iron wire twice around each potato and shape the far ends into small feet. Arrange the roses in the hollow potatoes.

TIP Potatoes are actually subterranean stems or tubers. That is why they belong to the chapter 'Stems & Branches'. This potato creation is a surprising table arrangement for an original party!

Cut the Polygonum vines into 2 cm strips. Bind them with wire into a graceful composition. Finish with Sedum.

Dried Polygonum/Japanese knotweed vines

Sedum

Floral wire

Composition with Polygonum

Young stems of Phragmites communis/reed

Rosa 'Green'

Reed leaves and stems with plumes

Plastic tubes

Iron wire

2 x 50 cm of floral stem wire

Reinforcing bars

Iron stand

Reed Stem Stand

Wire reed stems of 25 cm each on two pieces of floral stem wire, so you obtain two reed mats. With a reinforcing bar, make a horizontal axis on an iron stand. Attach the water-filled plastic tubes to the axis. Completely cover the axis with the reed mats. Arrange the roses in the tubes. Create a background with rolled reed leaves and stems with plumes. Fix everything with iron wire.

TIP Create a waving movement of the reed mats on the axis of the iron stand.

Hedera Balloons

Bind some 30 ivy vines around an inflated balloon. Firmly fix the far ends with spool wire. Let this dry for two weeks. Then, burst the balloon and remove the wire. Wrap the far ends again with spool wire and coloured cotton thread. Decorate the inside of this creation with polystyrene foam spheres, wrapped in cotton thread. Fix the thread with spray glue.

Hedera helix/ivy vines

Cotton thread (different colours)

Polystyrene foam spheres

Spool wire

Spray glue

Balloons

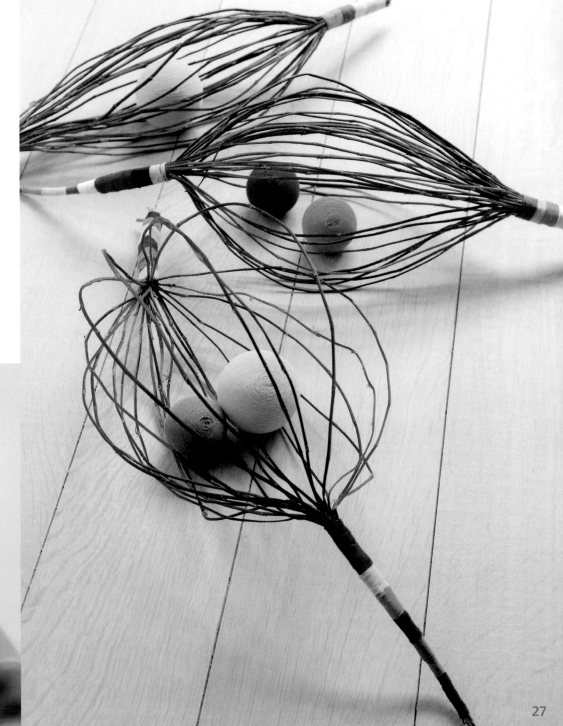

Wisteria sinensis

Dahlia 'Pompon'

Metal floral wire

Wisteria Butterflies

Remove the leaves from the Wisteria vines. Shape 14 vines
into loops. Wrap the far ends of the loops with metal floral wire.
Let the butterflies dry for two weeks. Then, remove the wire.
Bind firmly again turning only once around the ends and decorate
the binding point with a Dahlia 'Pompon'.

TIP You can also make this creation with Hedera vines.

Euphorbia canariensis/Canary Island Spurge stems (a cactus species)

Vanda 'Blue Magic'

Floral wire

Hollow out the dry Euphorbia canariensis stems and cut them into equal pieces with a fretsaw. Bind them to a garland with floral wire. Fill this garland with Vanda 'Blue Magic'.

Pond Phantasy with Euphorbia

A few branches of Macleaya cordata/plume poppy

10 branches of Delphinium 'El Barbablue'/larkspur

Flexible aluminium wire

2 glass vases

Plume Poppy Wave

Make a mat of plume poppy branches by double-binding the aluminium wire. Work at different heights. Arrange the flowers in the glass vases in between the wave of branches.

Make a Christmas tree out of cane ribbon that you bind with floral wire. Fix everything onto a bamboo stick with strong gold thread. Provide the stick with a horizontal bamboo axis at 60 cm from the bottom. Improve the shape of the Christmas tree with cane ribbon, fixed with staples. String the pearls onto the paper ribbon, reinforced with iron wire, and add them to the creation along with the Christmas lights.
Place the tree in a pot, filled with sand. Let the horizontal bamboo stick rest on the edge of the pot.

Pulp Cane Christmas Tree

Bleached narrow and wide cane ribbons

Strong gold thread

Floral wire

White paper ribbon, reinforced with iron wire

Big pearls

Christmas lights

Stapler

2 Bambusa/bamboo sticks

Sand

Pot (Mobach)

Dry stems of:

Sedum spectabile/sedum

Chelone obliqua/rose turtlehead

Hosta sieboldiana

Christmas baubles

Strong paper

Chicken wire

Glitter thread

Hot glue (glue gun)

Powder snow

3 metal rings

(diameters: 40 cm, 50 cm, 60 cm)

Christmas Basket of Stems

Stretch a piece of chicken wire into a tub shape on the backside of the three metal rings (that are welded together). Cover the chicken wire with strong paper ribbon. Glue the stems onto the paper. Fill the metal rings with dry stems and fix these with glue. Fill the basket with Christmas baubles. Finish with powder snow and glitter thread.

Festive Birch Bark Cake

Pile up the seven pieces of Betula papyrifera bark. Glue them together with two wood cubes. Keep a distance of 1.5 cm between the bark layers. Drill a hole in the layers to insert the plastic pipette. Fill each layer with a different material: dry pepper berries, dry Tillandsia usneoides, sheep's wool, Iceland moss and sisal. Fix these materials each time with cold glue. Fill the pipette with water and finish the composition with an orchid.

7 pieces of Betula papyrifera/
paper birch bark (10 x 10 cm)

Dry Schinus molle/pepper berries

Dry Tillandsia usneoides/Spanish moss

Sheep's wool

Cetratia islandica/Iceland moss

Sisal

Wood glue

Cold glue

12 little wood cubes

Plastic pipette

Orchid

TIP You can fill up this creation in different ways, according to season. A walk in the countryside will yield a treasure throve of materials that you can dry for use later.

Leaves & Grasses

Leaves are composed of flat slices with leafstalks. The plants absorb the sun's energy through the leaves, providing their environment with oxygen and food. Grasses are perennials with narrow, long leaves. They often have tiny little flowers in clusters or spikes. Mother Nature offers floral artists interested in making arrangements with leaves and grasses a wide range of possibilities, as they will discover surprising variations in the shape or the nerves, an endless diversity of species, and a rich colour palette.

Hosta sieboldiana

Bouquet of Hosta Leaves

Bind some 40 Hosta leaves into a sheaf, creating a natural bouquet.

Terrace Creation with Butterbur Stems

80 Petasites hybridus/butterbur stems

35 flower stems of different kinds of Hosta:

Hosta crispula, Hosta decorata, Hosta sieboldiana

Floral foam

Concrete plate

Arrange the butterbur stems and
the Hosta flower stems alternately
on a square piece of wet floral foam.
Finish the visible floral foam with
a few layers of leafstalks.
Bind everything tightly together with
the epidermis of butterbur leafstalks.

TIP Make sure that the closed Hosta
buds nicely stick out over the cut off
leafstalks.

Butterbur Cocoons

Petasites hybridus/butterbur

Anthurium 'Snowy'/flamingo flower

Pipettes

Roll the butterbur inwards so you obtain a cocoon shape.
Sew up the cocoon with the upper skin of the leafstalk.
Use a darning needle. Create an arrangement with
approximately 20 cocoons. Finish with Anthurium
'Snowy'. Use your imagination! Place every flower in
a water-filled pipette.

Maize Leaf Towers

Zea mays/maize leaves

Stand with 2 thin iron bars

Fold a maize leaf from the wide to the narrow side into an accordion. Stick the folded leaf with the main nerve on the iron bar. Build at the same time two maize leaf towers, from wide to narrow. Leave sufficient space between both structures.

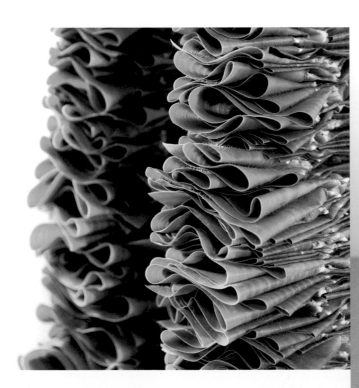

Xanthorrhoea/steel grass

Morus nigra/black mulberries

(berries available in different colours)

TIP Let children help you make this arrangement. It is a fun experience for a birthday party or a baby shower!

Coffeepot filled with Steel Grass

String mulberry berries on steel grass. Place them at different heights and use different colours. Create a playful arrangement in the coffeepot.

Table Arrangement with Cordyline Leaves

Cut the top and the base of all the Cordyline fruticosa 'Black Tie' leaves. Glue two leaves together with their main nerves touching each other, so you obtain a large backbone. Make an incision up to the main nerve every 8 cm. Cut the other four leaves into 7 cm pieces. Cut the main nerve out of every leaf up to 2 cm from the edge. Pull these pieces over the cuts in the backbone. Decorate the cases with Viburnum opulus berries. Present the composition on a ceramic plate.

6 Cordyline fruticosa 'Black Tie' leaves

Viburnum opulus/guelder rose berries

Cold glue

Ceramic plate

Flower Shape of Cordyline Leaves

Arrange the Cordyline leaf tips
around the basket of the stand.
Let the leaves end on the metal wire.
Fix with floral wire. Decorate with
Viburnum opulus berries.

Cordyline fruticosa 'Black Tie' leaves

(2 tips of 25 cm each)

Viburnum opulus/guelder rose berries

Brick-red floral thread

Stand with metal wire and basket

TIP Store the cut grasses a week before you make the arrangement in a dry, dark place so the excess humidity can evaporate.

Luzula Cushion

Make knots on the chicken wire, using seven leaves of Luzula grass and one raffia for each knot. Repeat this every two or three openings until the surface is totally covered. Arrange Spathiphyllum between every two knots, so you obtain a circle.

Luzula sylvatica/wood rush

White Raphia farinefera/raffia

20 Spathiphyllum/peace lilies

Plastified chicken wire

(30 x 30 cms – with 1.2 cm openings)

Aspidistra leaf

Bleached pulp cane

Cold glue

Transparent double-sided tape

Garden Fable with Aspidistra Leaf

Create a little pointed hat with the Aspidistra by turning it around the midrib. Fix the overlap with glue. Fold the remaining part of the leaf inwards in the arrangement and fix it with double-sided tape. Hang the hat over a pulp cane.

Roll the banana leaf in a circle. Fix with floral wire. Arrange the double-folded Japanese creeper leaves into the circle. Glue the far end. Finish the creation with a beautiful rose.

Eternal Love with Musa Acuminata

Bleached Musa acuminata/banana leaf

Parthenocissus tricuspidata 'Veitchii'/Japanese creeper leaves

Rosa 'Red Naomi'

Floral wire

Hot glue (glue gun)

25 Miscanthus sinensis/Eulalia Grass

12 fresh Lilium 'White Heaven'/lilies

Binding wire

Grave Bouquet with Eulalia Grass

Remove the tough main stem of the Eulalia grass up to the middle. Create half hearts with the grass around the remaining main stem. Fix each time with binding wire. Wrap the bottom of the main stem with grass. Clasp the lilies with their stems at the central binding point.

TIP Fresh lily buds can stay fresh without water for several days.

52

Leafstalks of Parthenocissus tricuspidata 'Veitchii'/Japanese creeper

Pigment (iron oxide red)

White cement

White sand

Water

Make 16 concrete blocks (9 x 9 cm each) of white cement, white sand and a little bit of water. Add some pigment to this mixture. Arrange the Japanese creeper leafstalks in the wet concrete, forming characters of your choice.

Poetry of Japanese Creeper

TIP This technique allows you to give shape to a poem or other text you like. Of course you can also write the poem yourself!

Populus alba/white poplar leaves

Fast plaster

Water

Piece of cardboard

Wooden mould (12 x 12 cm / 3 cm high)

First, design your figuration with white poplar leaves on a piece of cardboard. Make a mixture of fast plaster and water. Pour this mixture into the wooden mould. Press your design into the plaster. Let it dry.

Wall Tiles of White Poplar

TIP This creation offers an endless range of possibilities. With pieces of leaves or leafstalks, you can create any shape you like: circles, triangles, lines, etc. A beautiful arrangement to give away or to receive!

Musa acuminata/banana leaf

Gold leaf

2 thin elastic bands

Banana Leaf Bracelet

Cut the banana leaf into strips of 2.5 cm wide and 7.5 cm long. Wire the strips one by one at two points on the elastic bands. Decorate the edges of the leaf here and there with gold leaf.

Knit a 2.5 x 30 cm piece of flexigrass. Remove the knitting needles and fix the
loops on the topside tightly with little glass pearls, wired on thin silver thread.
Do the same thing on the bottom, but more whimsically this time.

Fairylike Flexigrass Jewel

Flexigrass

Glass pearls

Fine knitting needles

Thin silver thread

Fibres

Fibres form the cell material of every plant. The thin, filiform parts can be removed from the plant by different methods including tearing, pulling, soaking, or washing. Floral designers with an eye for the plant's structure like to give fibres the leading part in their works.

Knit pieces of flax fibre with knitting needles no. 7. Knit alternately loosely and tightly. Knit the flax fibre pieces together until you obtain a loose bag. Fill the bag with walnuts. Attach the bag to the pulp cane triangle and hang this in the vase.
Finish with a wig of wired Hydrangea arborescens 'Annabelle' tufts.

Knitting with Flax Fibre

Ball of Linum usitatissimum/flax fibre

Juglans regia/walnut (in shell)

Hydrangea arborescens 'Annabelle'

Binding wire

Pulp cane

Knitting needles no. 7

Glass vases

Kissing Carnations in Raffia

Crochet the raffia fibres into a 1 m x 7 cm piece. At the end, add a small piece of 20 x 15 cm. Wrap the crocheted fibres around the stand. Form a funnel on top of the ring. Sew everything tightly together with raffia. Bind the carnations into a short bouquet and arrange them in the funnel, previously covered with plastic film and filled with water.

Raphia farinefera/raffia fibres

Dianthus 'Ganache'/carnation

(20 per arrangement)

Crochet hook no. 7

Binding wire

Plastic film

Stand with a ring on the top

Bleached Raphia farinefera/raffia

Morus nigra/mulberry fibre

Merinos wool

Silk

Cotton (balls and fibre)

Skeleton fibre of Ficus benjamina/weeping fig

Cold glue

Deciduous tree branches (1 m long)

Mantelpiece Arrangement with Fibres

Wrap the different fibres tightly around a branch. Fix the far ends with cold glue. Make a garland of cotton balls on a branch and bind the balls with fibres.

TIP This mantelpiece arrangement is a wonderful, alternative Christmas decoration.

End leaves of Zea mays/maize (cob)

Skeleton fibre of Ficus benjamina/weeping fig

Fibre of Morus nigra/black mulberry

Combed and uncombed wool

Dry Clematis seed fluffs

Gold and silver thread

Gold and silver stars

Enamelled floral wire

Gold and silver spray paint

Populus alba/white poplar branches

Clay brick

Christmas Trees with Fibres

Create the base shape of a Christmas tree with enamelled floral wire. Cover the base with one of the fibres. Wrap with gold or silver thread. Fix a little tree with a Populus alba branch in a clay brick, previously painted with spray paint. Place a star on top of each tree.

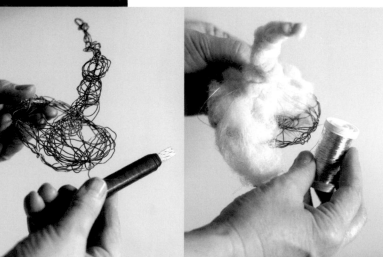

Elderberry Umbels

Make an iron wire lattice within the square, formed by the stands. Clasp dry umbels of Sambucus nigra between the iron wire. Glue fresh elderberries onto the creation. Finish with pearls, and pieces of hand-made paper.

Dry umbels and

fresh berries of

Sambucus nigra/elderberries

Hand-made paper

Pearls

Fine iron wire

Spray glue

2 metal stands

Flowers

Flowers are the plant's reproductive organ. They are usually composed of a calyx, corolla, stamens, and pistil. In nature flowers play the role of real seducers, drawing attention by their shapes, colours and fragrances. These eye-catchers from the plant world awaken our longing for floral design and beauty.

Hyacinthus 'Aiolos'/hyacinth

Dry Solanum tuberosum roots/potatoes

Flat moss

Paper ribbon (1 m)

Chicken wire

Cold glue

Plastic film

Floral wire

Spring Basket with Hyacinths

Glue the clean potato roots on the paper ribbon. Leave 3 cm free on both ends of the ribbon. Glue the far ends together into a circle. Make a chicken wire bottom for this structure. Fix with floral wire. Cover with plastic film. Arrange moist flat moss in the basket. Finally, arrange the hyacinths.

TIP The potato roots must be thoroughly dry before you clean them with a rough brush.

80 Muscari/grape hyacinths

Pinus pinaster/maritime pine needles

Double-sided tape (2 m)

Water-resistant tape

Miniature Arrangement with Muscari

Arrange bundles of maritime pine needles parallelly on double-sided tape. Press firmly. Arrange a bunch of Muscari. Fix well with water-resistant tape. Wrap the Muscari bunch with the band of maritime pine needles.

Bend the chicken wire into a cylinder with a 20 cm diameter. Fix with iron wire. Bend the wire on the bottom outwards for the base. Finish all the edges of the chicken wire on the top and on the bottom with iron wire. Arrange wet balls of cushion moss on the bottom of the vase. Lay every tulip on a leaf and roll into a cylinder shape. Fix the leaf with a pin. Arrange everything on the cushion moss in the vase.

Transparent Vase with Tulips

45 Tulipa 'Inzell'/tulips

Tulip leaves

5 balls of Leucobryum glaucum/cushion moss

Heavy chicken wire (60 cm wide – 75 cm long)

Silver-coloured pins

Iron wire

TIP Pierce the tulip stems with the pins when you fix the leaf tubes to avoid the flowers from growing.

Insert four thin iron bars into the corners of a clay brick. Build a container of reed stems around the iron bars (see 'Whirling Structure with Prairie Sunflower' in the chapter 'Stems & Branches' for the technique). Start binding at 25 cm height. Bind the stems with floral wire. Cover the reed container with Euonymus alata branches. Clasp and glue them.
The branches' rough structure must stay visible. Remove the clay. Bend the iron bars to form 'small feet'. Place five plastic tubes, previously wrapped in floral ribbon, in the container. Bind them together and to the container with floral wire and fill them with water.
Arrange the guelder rose and the turban buttercups.

Intimate Meeting with Guelder Rose

Viburnum opulus/guelder rose
Ranunculus 'Green Success'/turban buttercup
Bare branches of Euonymus alata/spindle tree
Phragmites/reed stems
Floral wire
4 thin iron bars (2.5 mm thick – 1 m high)
5 plastic tubes
Floral ribbon
Hot glue (glue gun)
Floral clay brick

Anemone 'Jerusalem Red'/anemone

Gerbera mini 'Burgundy'/gerbera

Pistacia lentiscus/mastic tree

Freeze-dried leaves of Buddleja davidii/butterfly bush

Crêpe paper (brick-red)

Stitching thread

Silk paper (red)

Extra strong glue pen

Romantic Bouquet with Anemone and Gerbera

Stitch the freeze-dried butterfly bush leaves together with a sewing machine. Make two bands of leaves. Put the bands on silk paper and stitch them vertically into a leaf sheet. Create a sheaf bouquet with anemone, gerbera and Pistacia lentiscus. Wrap the bouquet in the leaf sheet. Finish the creation with a crêpe paper edging and bow. Fix with the glue pen.

50 Ranunculus/turban buttercups:
'Elegance pink', 'Elegance pastel',
'Elegance white', 'Success pink'
Coloured pulp cane
Flat moss
Chicken wire
Plastic film
Floral foam
Iron wire
Double-sided tape

TIP If you are looking for a nice table arrangement, you can also make this creation with smaller dimensions.

Turban Buttercup Symphony

For the front side: place twelve pieces of pulp cane on double-sided tape: ten pieces of 10 cm and two pieces of 60 cm. Roll the tape into a bundle and fix with iron wire. Attach all bundles to a container of strong chicken wire (7 cm wide – 60 cm long – 8 cm high). For the sides: place twelve pieces of pulp cane (60 cm long) on double-sided tape. Attach these bundles to the container as well. Fill the chicken wire with flat moss. Cover this with plastic film and wet floral foam. Arrange the turban buttercups with the capitulums above the pulp cane.

Paeonia lactiflora 'Sarah Bernhardt'/peony

Spun wool

Chicken wire

Conical plate (Mobach)

Peony Volcano

Bend a piece of chicken wire into a conical shape. Wrap it carefully with wool. Place the wooden shape on the plate and fill with water. Arrange the peonies in the middle.

TIP Give the chicken wire a nice, conical shape by making three big folds.

Ecological Rose Wreath

Mixture of Ecuadorian roses

Plastic bags (used packing)

Coloured chenille thread

Glass marbles

Pipettes

Coloured Raphia farinefera/raffia

Double metal ring

Wrap coloured raffia around the double metal ring. Fill the plastic bags with glass marbles. Reinforce the edge of each bag with coloured chenille thread. Arrange the bags on the ring like a wreath. Fill each bag with a colourful rose in a water-filled pipette.

Fiery Basket with Summer Flowers

Flowers:

Chelone obliqua/rose turtlehead

Polygonum amplexicaule/knotweed

Agapanthus 'Intermedius'/African lily

Achillea filipendulina/fernleaf yarrow

Nigella damascena 'Power Blue'/love-in-the-mist

Scabiosa caucasica/pincushion flower

Branches:

Sambucus nigra/elderberry

Fraxinus excelsior/common ash

Tilia x europaea/Dutch lime

Juglans regia/walnut

Salix alba/white willow

Alnus glutinosa/black alder

Seed capsules and fruits:

Papaver 'Pizzicato'

Alnus glutinosa/black alder

Euonymus europaeus/spindle tree

Viburnum opulus 'Notcutt'/guelder rose

Cast iron bucket

Iron wire

Staples

Fix a cast iron bucket on a wooden cross made of branches. Arrange a series of branches around the bucket. Fix them with iron wire and staples. Continue with two more series of branches. The four feet of the arrangement are part of the branches on the outside. Finish with a bouquet of flowers, seed capsules and fruits.

TIP You can fill this terrace arrangement with fresh flowers throughout the summer.

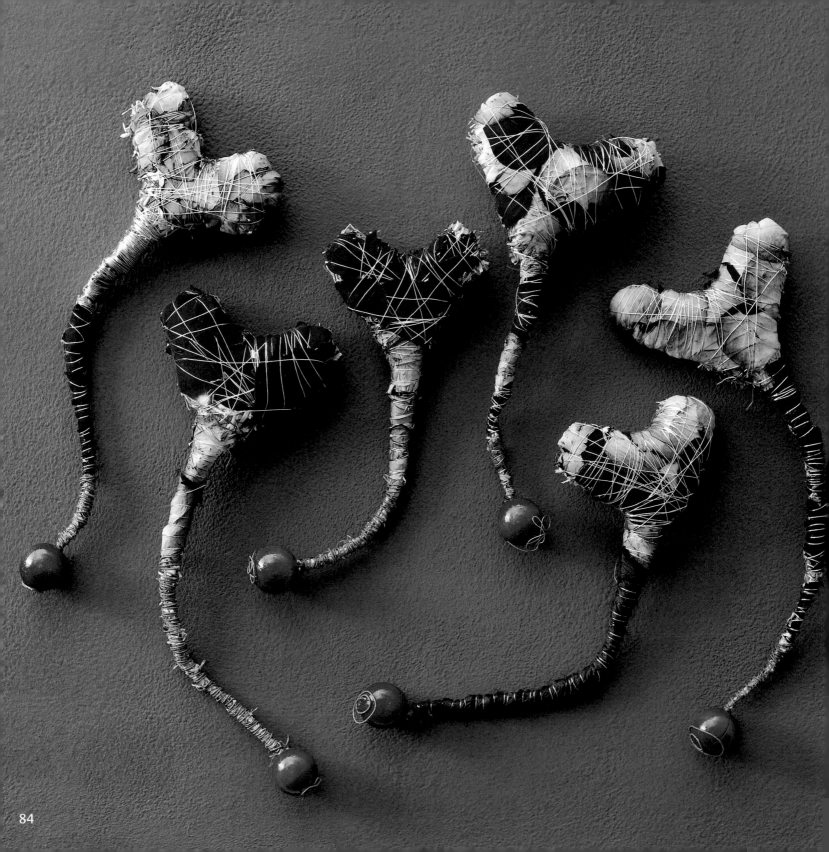

Fresh Rosa 'Ruby Red' petals

Hay

Red wooden bead

Red glitter thread

Fine silver thread

Red floral wire

Bind a hay bundle with red glitter thread making a heart. Make a long hay tail at the bottom of the heart. Refine the shape with scissors. Wrap the heart entirely in rose petals. Work in groups of three. Alternate the pink outside and the red inside. Bind each time with silver thread. Finish the tail with red floral wire. Use also red floral wire to attach the wooden bead.

Heart with Rose Petals

TIP Remove the leaf base from the rose petals to avoid breaking them while wrapping around the heart. If you don't have fresh rose petals, taffeta is a nice alternative.

Begonias

Wool

Cord

Coloured thread assortment:

cotton, silk, flax fibre, sisal

Metal base

Hammock with Begonias

Weave an imaginative mat with the different threads and the cord. Wrap the metal base in wool. Attach the mat to the base. Finish with begonias.

Rosa 'Mini Eden'

Scirpus/rush

Binding wire

Cord

Spool thread

Rose wire

River of Cluster Roses

First, make seven rush mats. Wire the rush together and fix every rush between two pieces of folded binding thread. Cut the edges of the mats to the same length. Fold the mats into a groove and slide them into each other. Make a garland of cluster roses and put it in the mats.

TIP Make a solid garland by wiring the cluster roses onto the rose thread. The flowers will dry nicely.

Chrysanthemum 'Britney'/chrysanthemum

Gypsophila paniculata 'Million Stars'/gypsophila

Mosaic composed of:

Glass

Skeleton leaf

Dry Betula/birch bark

Dry Musa acuminata/banana leaf

Dry Platanus x acerifolia/plane-tree leaf

Lunaria annua/honesty or money plant

Spray paint (gold)

Cold glue

Floral wire

Plastic film

Floral foam sphere

Box of recycled cardboard

Dowry with Chrysanthemums

Paint the cardboard box with gold spray paint. Cover it with the different mosaic materials. Use cold glue to fix them. Make tufts of gypsophila and bind them with floral wire. Fill the wet floral foam sphere completely with the tufts of gypsophila. Cover the bottom of the box with plastic film. Put the sphere with gypsophila on it. Finish the arrangement with previously wired chrysanthemums.

Place the wooden Larix segments against the back of the hearth. Fill the glass vases halfway with water, beads and sisal. Arrange them in between the larch segments. Fill three vases with a mixed Amaryllis bouquet, bound with cord. Finish the arrangement with glitter thread.

Hearthglow of Amaryllis

Amaryllis 'Christmas',
'Red Lion', 'La Paz', 'Chico',
'Royal Velve', 'Ambiance'
6 triangular segments of
Larix decidua/larch
Red beads
Red sisal
Red glitter thread
Red cord
5 little glass vases

TIP Cover the visible floral pins with plane-tree leaves. Use cold glue to fix them.

Soak the floral foam wreath in water until it has absorbed enough water. Remove the mesophyll from the plane-tree leaves and keep only the leafstalks and ribs. Tightly wrap this around the wreath with floral wire. Then, pass a wired pearl through the tube at the end of each plane-tree leafstalk. Attach them all on the inside and outside of the wreath with floral pins. This way, you will obtain a circle of pearls and a network of ribs. Arrange the Helleborus in the composition.

Winter Wreath with Helleborus

30 Helleborus niger/Christmas rose

Dry Platanus x acerifolia/plane-tree leaf

Floral foam wreath (35 cm diameter)

Wired pearls

Floral wire

Floral pins

Floral Aid with Zantedeschia

Connect the two double metal rings (the big one on top) with four vertical metal bars making a floral aid. Arrange the Zantedeschia between the rings of the floral aid. It is important that the stems can take up enough water from the ceramic plate.

50 Zantedeschia 'Avalanche'/arum

Floral aid:

1 horizontally welded double metal ring
(30 and 25 cm diameter)

1 horizontally welded double metal ring
(35 and 30 cm diameter)

4 thin metal bars

Ceramic plate

TIP You can ask an experienced welder to make a floral aid any size you want. Fill it in different ways with seasonal flowers throughout the year.

Fruits
& Seeds

Fruits and seeds carry life inside them.
They guarantee the continuation of their
species. Florists consider the enormous
variety of local fruits and seeds, and the
increasing range of foreign species, as a
valuable treasure of creative materials.

Papaver somniferum/poppy

Wooden shelf

Ecoline paint

Still Life with Papaver

Treat a wooden shelf with ecoline paint. Cut Papaver seed capsules in two at different heights.
This way, you will obtain small vases that you can arrange alternately by putting either the
crowns or the base of the capsule on the wooden shelf making it into a pure still life.

Bouquet with Papaver Seed Capsules

Papaver somniferum/poppy

Xerophyllum tenax/bear grass

Glass vase

Bind a playful bouquet with approximately 15 papaver seed capsules. Surround them with bear grass. Let the leaf tops swing into the glass vase.

TIP Before you start arranging, wash the bear grass thoroughly with warm water and soap.

Papaver somniferum/poppy

Floral wire

Caterpillar of Papaver Seed Capsules

Bind Papaver seed capsules together, attaching alternately the bottom left and the bottom right with floral wire. Bind them here and there for a second time at the stems. The result will be a sturdy caterpillar.

Winged fruits of Tilia x europaea/Dutch lime

Winding wire with fine green cloth

Beads or pearls

4 conical glass vases

Window Poem
with Lime Fruits

Cover the top of the glass vases with winding wire. Create a playful clothesline between the vases. Finish the far ends of the threads on the first and the last vase with beads or pearls. Hang the lime fruits over the thread.

Bride's Greeting with Sallow Seed Fluffs

TIP Zantedeschia is much more flexible if you take it out of the water a day before you make your arrangement.

Salix caprea/sallow seed fluffs

Nepalese paper

Zantedeschia 'Blush'/arum

Pipettes

Make eight little boxes out of Nepalese paper. Fill them with clean sallow seed fluffs. Place the Zantedeschia in a water-filled pipette. Arrange the flowers in pairs in the boxes. Finish with sallow seed fluffs.

Make cubes of wet garden mould. Let them dry. Hollow each cube out with a knife. Bind the Malus apples with glitter thread. Arrange them imaginatively into the cubes.

Malus apples

Garden mould

Flexible red glitter thread

Autumn Evocation with Malus Apples

TIP You can also use clay instead of garden mould.

Bellgums/tropical fruit boxes

Heracleum sphondylium/hogweed stems

Hydrangea macrophylla/hydrangea

Thin wooden strip

Hot glue (glue gun)

TIP Be careful when you pick the hogweed. The sap from this plant contains a poisonous substance. When it is combined with sunlight, it reacts like an acid that can cause serious skin damage. You can also use Polygonum (Japanese knotweed) stems instead of hogweed.

Vases with Bellgums

Cut hogweed stems lengthwise with a fretsaw. Glue stems of approximately 15 cm in the middle of a flat wooden strip. Arrange the stems alternately with the inside and the outside upwards. Clasp the Bellgums in the stem cavities. Finish with hydrangea.

Farewell with Callicarpa Berries

Cut the Salix purpurea bundles to the same length and bind them with nylon thread. Arrange them in the shape of two valleys and attach them crosswise to each other with two wooden sticks. Place the Zantedeschia in water-filled plastic tubes. Arrange them elegantly in the Salix valleys. Fix with tape where needed. Finish the creation with Callicarpa berries.

Callicarpa bodinieri 'Profusion'/beauty berries

3 bundles of Salix purpurea/purple willow

12 Zantedeschia 'Schwarzwalder'/arum

Nylon thread

2 wooden sticks

Water-resistant tape

Plastic tubes

Papaver somniferum/poppy
(corollas, profiles and bases
of the seed capsules)
3 square wooden frames
(colour of your choice)
Wooden strips (same colour)
Cold glue

Make a square from the wooden strips and place them in the middle of the wooden frames. Fill the squares generously with Papaver seed capsules: the first one with corollas, the second with profiles, and the third one with bases. Fix them well with glue.

Triptych with Papaver

Give the perforated seed capsules 'small feet' made from pulp cane. Create an arrangement with the seed capsules. Fill with different kinds of fruits and seeds.

Fruits and seeds of:

Callicarpa bodinieri 'Profusion'/beauty berries

Euonymus europaeus/spindle tree

Symphoricarpos albus/snowberries

Skimmia japonica 'Veitchii'/Japanese skimmia

Osmanthus heterophyllus/false holly

Agapanthus/African lily

Pulp cane

Perforated Bell Cup/African seed capsules

Fruits and Seeds Cocktail

Autumn Arrangement with Great Reed Mace

Bend the metal frame making a plate. Stick the great reed mace leaf on the bottom of the frame. Arrange the great reed mace seed capsules parallelly. Fix the far ends with glue. Finish with chestnuts, clasped between an elongated ball of rusty iron wire and tropical nuts, wired onto a brown glitter thread. Cover the frame feet with great reed mace stems.

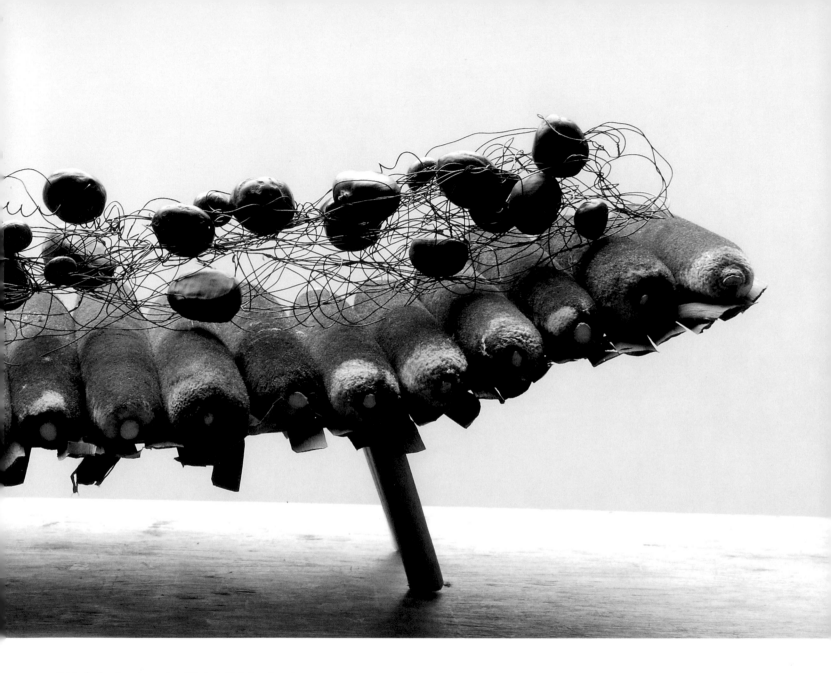

Stems, leaf and seed capsules of Typha latifolia/great reed mace

Castanea sativa/chestnut fruits

Tropical nuts

Rusty iron wire

Brown glitter thread

Cold glue

Rectangular metal frame with feet

Fruits and 3 thin branches of

Symphoricarpos albus/snowberry

Gypsophila paniculata/gypsophila

Spool thread

Nepalese paper

Stand filled with Salix fragilis Belgium Red/red crack willow

Snowberry Garland

Create a garland with bundles of snowberry and tufts of gypsophila on three thin snowberry branches. Bind them each time with spool thread. Attach the garland to a stand, filled with red crack willow. Finish the backside of the garland with a tube of Nepalese paper.

RITA VAN GANSBEKE, a biology teacher at the Sint-Franciscusinstituut in Melle (Belgium), has always been fascinated by the structure of plants. This interest encouraged her to take a master florist training course in Vught (The Netherlands). In 1997 Rita started 'Plantaardig beschouwd', a workshop where she organises vegetal design and floral art courses. Rita's greatest passion is to show what a professional or amateur florist can create with natural materials, and most importantly to transmit this beauty. This master florist enjoys the challenge of applying age-old techniques such as binding, heaping, wiring, etc. to contemporary floral art in an innovative way. Her style is natural, rhythmical and affectingly spontaneous. Her main sources of inspiration are nature, the garden, creative object development, and tendencies from the art and interior design world.

In this book Rita introduces you to her sublime floral art, the ultimate connection between natural materials, shapes and emotions.

PATRICIA DE CORTE is a poet and an author, famous for her remarkable poetry and flower arranging books 'Bloeiende woorden', 'De Zevensprong' and 'Rozen voor altijd'. She also writes much-appreciated contributions for the green guide in the VUM newspapers. In 'Fine Fleur', a book published for the 33rd edition of the Ghent Floraliën, she made a poetical portrait of the selected master florists, their creations, and the floral art schools.
She admires the sheer beauty in Rita Van Gansbeke's floral art, which has been an inspiring motivation to describe all the arrangements in the book with clarity and refinement.

ISABELLE PERSYN is a freelance photographer. Fine artistic expression and high-quality craftsmanship are some of the most distinguishing aspects of her talent. Isabelle has specialised in photographs about nature and life. Her images feature a sensitive connection between man and nature. She has contributed to several successful books on flower arranging including 'De Groene Verbeelding, een bloemstuk uit je eigen tuin', 'The Bouquet Talks', and 'Floristic Basics'. Isabelle seeks for perfection. The keywords in her work are simplicity, aesthetics and an eye for details. Her timeless photographs reveal the human warmth in Rita Van Gansbeke's floral art.

Special thanks

Willy

Hannelore, Chris, Maud and Simon

Willem, Sonia

Maarten

Mariette and family

Aline

An

Griet

Dany

Karel

Thanks for the location

Michel, Ria, Sofie and Louis

Father Walter - Listed presbytery (1750), Hillegem (BE)

Chapel of Kerselare (BE)

Nathalie, Krista - www.doublevoice.be

Campo Santo, Sint-Amandsberg (BE)

Jef, Lisbet, Louis and Charlotte

Thanks for the presentation

Count Renaud de Kerchove de Denterghem

www.parkvanbeervelde.be

A special present

May this book be a unique present
for all those who love natural beauty
and especially for **MAARTEN**.

Creations

Rita Van Gansbeke

Master Florist Vught

Plantaardig beschouwd

Cliviastraat 4

B-9820 Merelbeke (BE)

Tel. +32 9 362 88 30

rita.vangansbeke@telenet.be

Text and coordination

Patricia De Corte (BE)

PenDCommunications@telenet.be

Photography

Isabelle Persyn (BE)

www.isabellepersyn.com

Translation

Taal-Ad-Visie, Brugge

Final editing

Heide-Mieke Scherpereel

Layout and print

Group Van Damme bvba, Oostkamp (BE)

Published by

Stichting Kunstboek bvba

Legeweg 165

B-8020 Oostkamp (Belgium)

Tel. +32 50 46 19 10

Fax +32 50 46 19 18

info@stichtingkunstboek.com

www.stichtingkunstboek.com

ISBN: 978-90-5856-266-1

D/2008/6407/14

NUR: 421